Alamo

Lori Dittmer

Creative Education • Creative Paperbacks

Road map of

Contents

Welcome to the Alamo! It sits in downtown San Antonio, Texas. The Alamo has been used in many ways over the years.

In 1718, people built the **Mission** San Antonio de Valero. Spanish priests and American Indians lived there. The mission moved to its present location in 1724.

San Antonio
Texas

500 feet (152 m)
USA
Washington Monument
555 feet (169 m)
U.K.
Big Ben
315 feet (96 m)
USA
Statue of Liberty
305 feet (93 m)
250 feet (76.2 m)

How tall is the **Alamo chapel?**

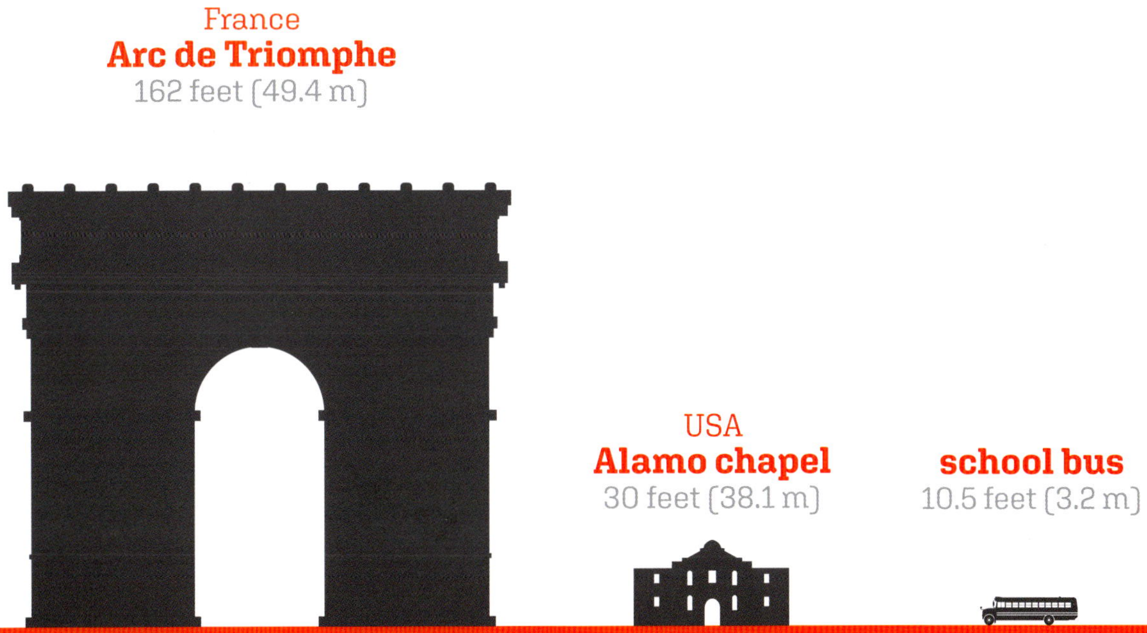

In the 1700s, Texas was part of Mexico. Spain controlled Mexico. For a while, Spanish soldiers lived at the mission. They called it *el Alamo* ("cottonwood") for the trees surrounding it.

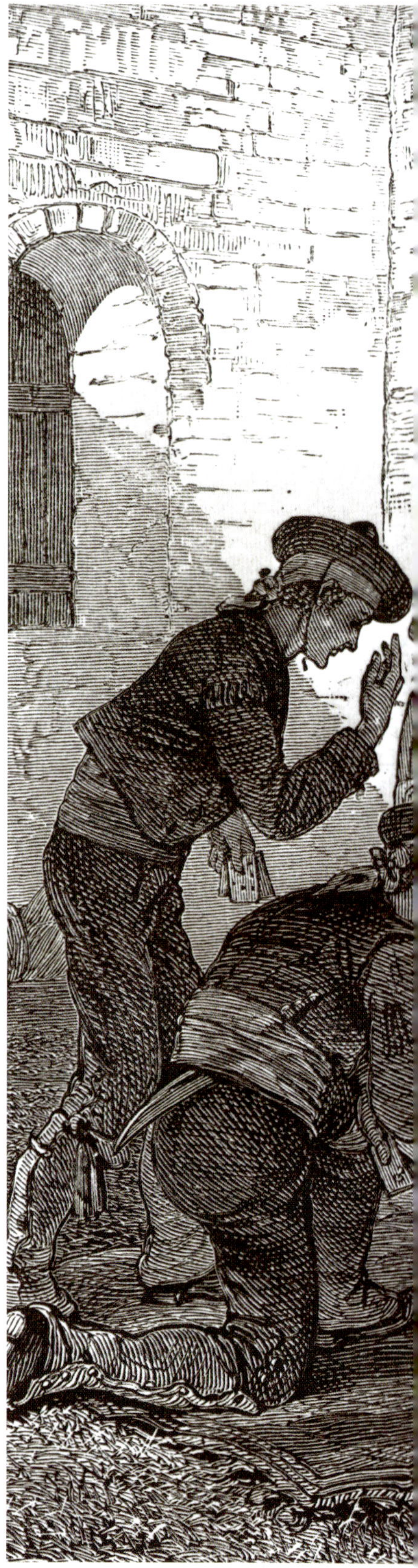

A famous battle took place at the Alamo in 1836. The church had become a Texas **fort**. Soldiers at the Alamo fought the Mexican army for 13 days. Mexico won. Weeks later, Texas gained its independence. In 1845, Texas joined the United States.

13  days

casualties

about 200 Alamo defenders

about 600 Mexican soldiers

The Alamo is a **compound**. In the 1800s, it covered about three acres (1.2 ha) of land. A wall surrounded it. Workers built the chapel with thick limestone blocks. Other buildings were made with mud bricks. The Alamo had **barracks**, a hospital, and a horse pen. Cannons sat along walls and atop buildings.

The Battle of the Alamo damaged the compound. After Texas became a state, the U.S. Army repaired the buildings. They added an arched rooftop to the chapel. Later, the Alamo became a **memorial**.

◄ Spirit of Sacrifice
- Alamo monument

More than 2.5 million people visit the Alamo each year. If you go, walk through the gardens. Explore the chapel. Read about its history.

Chapel
Centennial Museum

Nearby, tourists can stroll along the San Antonio River Walk. Four other missions were built along the river in the 1700s. You can visit all of them!

Can you spot these in the picture above?

The Alamo

St. Joseph Church

Tower of the Americas

★ Activity ★

Make a Mud Brick

materials

water

bowl

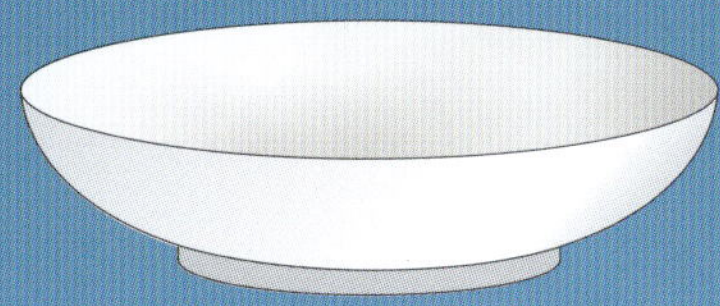

a mold

(such as the bottom of a small milk carton)

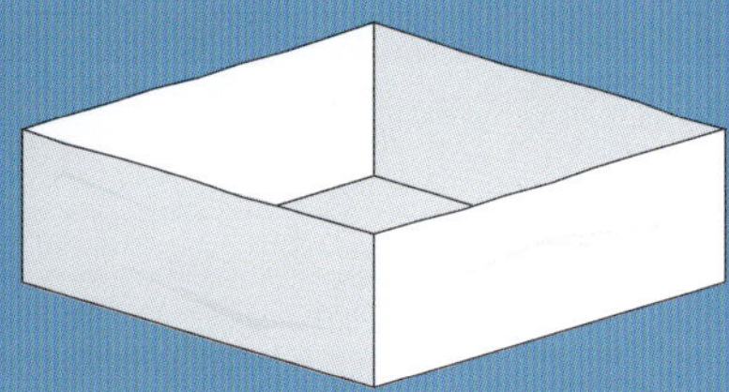

dried grass or straw

pieces shorter than 3 inches (7.6 cm)

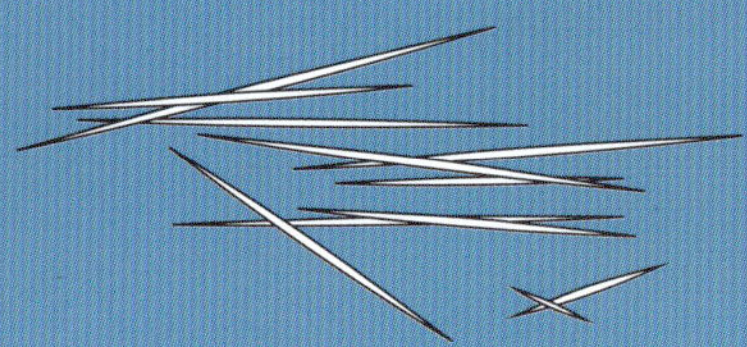

spoon

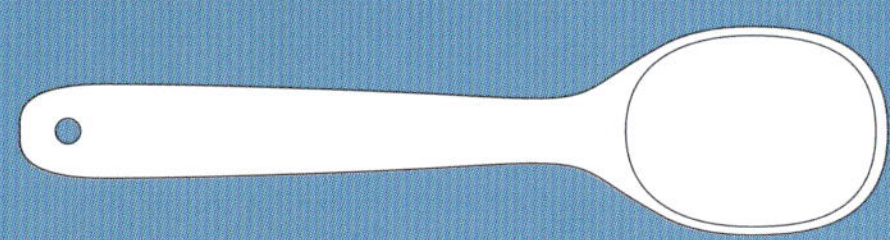

dirt

1

Put dirt and grass or straw in a bowl. Add water, and mix until a thick paste forms.

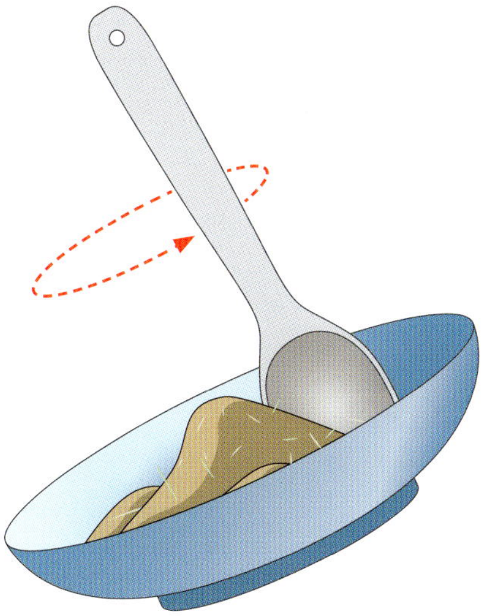

2

Fill the mold with the mixture. Pack it down.

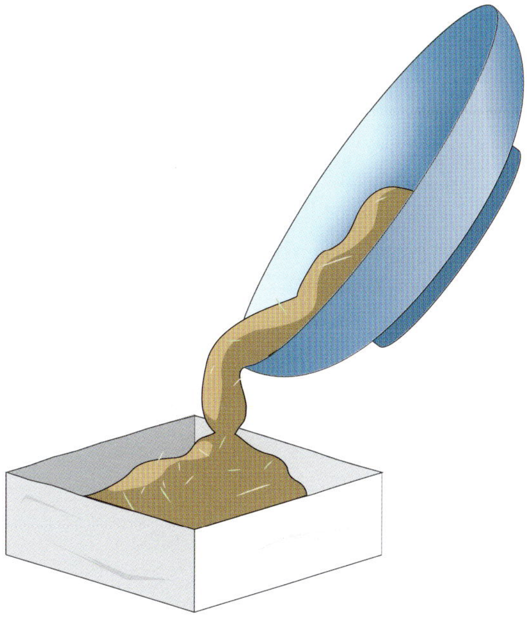

3

Put it by a sunny window or outside in the sun. Leave it to dry. This may take several days.

4

Peel off the carton. Place the brick in the shade to finish drying.

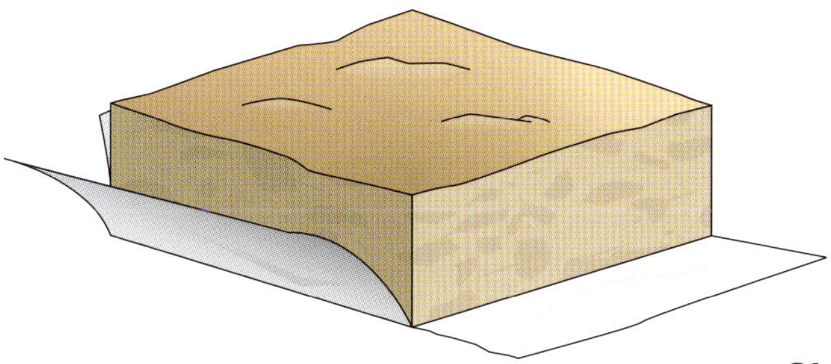

Glossary

barracks
a group of buildings used for housing soldiers

compound
a fenced or walled-in area that contains a group of buildings

fort
a strong building where soldiers stay to keep safe from an enemy

memorial
something that reminds people of a person or event

mission
a church and community founded by people who are sent to an area to share a religion

Read More

Nelson, Kristin L. *The Alamo*. Minneapolis: Lerner, 2011.

Peppas, Lynn. *The Battle of the Alamo*. New York: Crabtree, 2018.

Websites

The Alamo: Digital Battlefield Then and Now

See what the Alamo looked like in 1836, compared with how it looks today.

http://www.thealamo.org/remember/savethealamo/digitalbattlefield/index.html

Enchanted Learning: The Alamo

Read more about the history of the Alamo.

https://www.enchantedlearning.com/history/us/monuments/alamo/

Note: Every effort has been made to ensure that the websites listed above are suitable for children, that they have educational value, and that they contain no inappropriate material. However, because of the nature of the Internet, it is impossible to guarantee that these sites will remain active indefinitely or that their contents will not be altered.

Index

PUBLISHED BY CREATIVE EDUCATION AND CREATIVE PAPERBACKS
P.O. Box 227, Mankato, Minnesota 56002
Creative Education and Creative Paperbacks are imprints of The Creative Company
www.thecreativecompany.us

LIBRARY OF CONGRESS CATALOGING-IN-PUBLICATION DATA
Names: Dittmer, Lori, author.
Title: The Alamo / Lori Dittmer.
Series: Landmarks of America.
Includes bibliographical references and index.
Summary: Examining the building process from the ground up, this high-interest title covers the history and construction of the Alamo, one of Texas's most well-known landmarks.

LCCN: 2018061065
ISBN 978-1-64026-122-8 (hardcover)
ISBN 978-1-62832-685-7 (pbk)
ISBN 978-1-64000-240-1 (eBook)

Subjects: LCSH: Alamo (San Antonio, Tex.)—Juvenile literature. / Alamo (San Antonio, Tex.)—Siege, 1836—Juvenile literature.
Classification: LCC F390.D56 2019
DDC 976.4/03—dc23

DESIGN AND PRODUCTION
by Joe Kahnke; art direction by Rita Marshall
Printed in China

PHOTOGRAPHS by Alamy (George Ostertag), Bridgeman Images (Spanish Mission of the Alamo, from "The Romance of Tragedy of Pioneer Life," by Augustus L. Mason, 1883 [engraving], after Sheppard, William Ludlow [d.1912]/Private Collection), Getty Images (Holger Leue/Lonely Planet Images, Murat Taner/Photographer's Choice, Ed Vebell/Archive Photos), iStockphoto (Dean_Fikar, Pgiam), Shutterstock (BATKA, f11photo, Jellicle, Ritu Manoj Jethani, Ranier Lesniewski, Richard A McMillin, Sean Pavone, Philip Arno Photography, Piotr Przyluski, Alexey Pushkin, Dvorko Sergey)

FIRST EDITION HC 9 8 7 6 5 4 3 2 1
FIRST EDITION PBK 9 8 7 6 5 4 3 2 1